Chance'see ... with Me ☺

Devon Presha

To order additional copies of this book, contact:
Xlibris
1-888-795-4274
www.Xlibris.com
Orders@Xlibris.com

GOOD MORNING. I'M LOOKING FOR A HOME FOR A KITTEN THAT WAS BORN BLIND WITH LITTLE MITTENS.

DO YOU KNOW SOMEONE WHO CAN GIVE HER THE LOVE AND CARE SHE NEEDS?

WITH TIME SHE WILL BE ALL THAT SHE WAS BORN TO BE!

YES, I BELIEVE I DO KNOW SOMEONE WHO CAN HELP." ME! " ☺

I WILL BE ALL SHE NEEDS AND I WILL NAME HER CHANCE 'SEE.

THAT WAY SHE WILL SOMEDAY SEE. I WILL GIVE CHANCE 'SEE ALL THE LOVE SHE NEEDS. "GOD" SO HELP ME!

SO THEN, IT BEGAN .... THE JOURNEY OF CHANCE'SEE AND A PLAN.

I WILL FEED, LOVE AND TEACH CHANCE 'SEE ALL SHE NEEDS TO BE A HAPPY CAT.

SHE WILL GROW STRONG AND BE ALL THAT. I WILL ALWAYS HAVE
HER BACK. ☺ CHANCE'SEE AND ME.

I WILL WATCH AND SHOW HER THE THINGS SHE CAN'T SEE .... LOVE IS WHAT CHANCE 'SEE NEED.

I TOOK CHANCE'SEE TO THE VET .... TO GET HER HEALTH CHECKED.
AND OKAY THE VET SAID .... NOW HAVE A GOOD DAY.

WE WENT HOME AND BEGAN TO PLAY THE NIGHT AWAY. ☺

Poem:

CHANCE'SEE

I AM GOING TO LEAD BY EXAMPLE.

I HAVE ADOPTED A KITTEN THAT CAN'T SEE

I WILL BE HER EYE'S...

YOU CAN TRUST IN ME.

GIVING HER THE CHANCE TO SEE THROUGH ME.

I HAVE A FRIEND, ALWAYS .....

CHANCE'SEE AND ME.

THIS BOOK IS DEDICATED TO:

ADELE PRESHA

LINDSEY ATKINS

ABDOUR SHABAZZ

THELMA PRESHA

ROY AND EVA ATKINS

MY HOST OF FAMILY AND FRIENDS.

ALL THE GREAT AUTHORS AND EDITORS WHO PAVED THE WAY BEFORE ME.

I GIVE THANKS-APPRECIATION AND MY LOVE. THANK YOU.

Printed in the United States
By Bookmasters